The Magic Pear Tree

Retold by Cheryl Stroud
Illustrated by Jean and Mou-sien Tseng

Celebration Press
An Imprint of Pearson Learning

There once was a farmer who grew juicy pears. When his pears were ripe, he filled his cart and went to town to sell them.

One day a poor man came to the farmer's cart.
"You have many pears," the man said.
"May I have one?"

"Go away. You have no money," the farmer said.

But the man wouldn't go away. The farmer began to yell at him. Soon people gathered around and told the farmer he was mean.

The poor man shook his head and said, "It's better to be kind. You'll see."

A woman handed the man a penny. The poor
man thanked her and bought a pear.

He ate the juicy pear, and kept one small seed. "This is all I need," he said.

Then he dug a hole, planted the seed, covered it with dirt, and watered it.

The crowd watched as a tiny green plant pushed through the dirt and grew into a tree full of juicy pears. The people couldn't believe their eyes!

11

The poor man picked the pears and gave them all away to the townspeople.

When the farmer turned to look at his cart, all his pears were gone!

The greedy farmer watched the townspeople
enjoy his juicy pears.